WELCOME TO
AMERICA
MICHAEL HEATH

WELCOME TO
AMERICA

MICHAEL HEATH

VIEW FROM CHELSEA HOTEL N.Y

HEINEMANN · LONDON

In memory of
Thelonious Monk

William Heinemann Ltd
10 Upper Grosvenor Street, London W1X 9PA
LONDON MELBOURNE TORONTO
JOHANNESBURG AUCKLAND

First published 1985

434 31425 0

Printed in Great Britain by
Redwood Burn Limited, Trowbridge, Wiltshire

ARRIVAL

WELCOME TO AMERICA

TICKETS TO N.Y
HOLLYWOOD
TICKETS TO LA
DALLAS
WASHINGTON
PANIC!
PANIC!
PANIC!
IF LOST RETURN TO PUNCH
GATE 37
TOO LATE!
ROAIR
SALT LAKE CITY
TICKETS TO DALLAS
LAS VEGAS
OVER COME FEAR OF FLYING
TICKETS TO NY

FLYING
IN A
747
DOWNTOWN →
UPTOWN →
HIGHLIFE
HOW TO
SURVIVE
CRASH

ALASKA
DELTA
DELTA
WESTERN
US
TRAVELLING
AROUND
AMERICA
BY PLANE

AIRPORT
FUN WITH
LUGGAGE

HOTEL
LOBBY LIVING

NEW YORK

WELOME TO
NEW YORK
NO WAY
POLICE

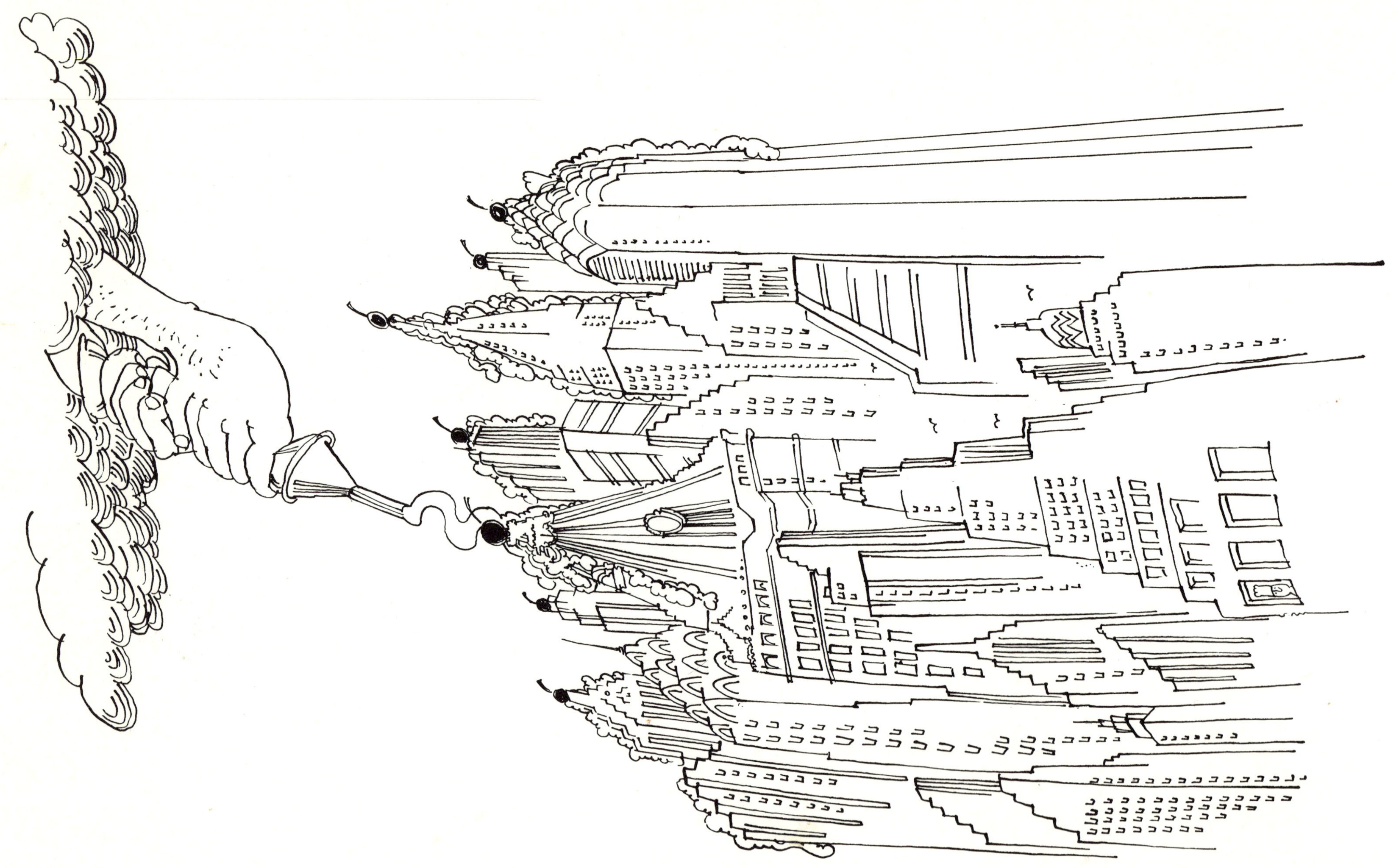

YOU'D COME UP HERE TOO—IF YOU'D SEEN WHAT IT WAS LIKE DOWN THERE!
HAVE A NICE DAY!!
GET A DOCTOR!!
WEEEEEEEE
BUY! BUY! BUY
ARRRGG! BAM! BAM! BAM!
WEEWEEEE!
OH MY GAAD MY HEART!
MY NAME'S BIFF!
GOT ANY SMALL CHANGE, FRIEND?
BLABLABLABLA
BUY! BUY! BUY! BUY!
POW!
SUCCESS! SUCCESS!
WELCOME TO RICH AND FAMOUS
IT'EM UP PUNK!
WEEEEEEE
REMEMBER
KILLS!

Marlboro
OK
SUCK
SEX
TALK DIRTY
LIVE SEX
PEEP BOOTHS
25¢
TALK DIRTY

HE ASKED ME THE WAY TO HIS HOTEL
HOW TO UNDER-STAND AMERICAN
SONY
Enjoy
FINE
?
New York

McDonald's
HAMBURGERS
HAPPY BIRTHDAY
I SEE YOU HAVE McDONALD'S OVER HERE AS WELL

ONEWAY
NO PARKING
DON'T WALK
7
W 23RD
HONK!
BARB!!
HONK!
WE BAILED YOU OUT OF THE FIRST GODAWFUL WAR AN' WE BAILED YOU OUT OF THE SECOND GOD DAMMIT!
TAXI
WHAT THE FUCK!
NY 123341
NY 12334
POTHOLES N.Y

GO FOR IT!
LOVE YOUR MOTHER
NEW YORK
SLY MIDGET
FOOLS
BLIND
COUPLE

SUBWAY ART

HOTEL
MOTEL
LONDON GIN
STEAKS
WHISKEY
CAFE
BEER
SEX
DENTIST
EATS
DELI
INN
WEIGHT LOSS
SONY
BURGER
BAR
HOT DOGS
SMOKE
TRAVEL
EL CHARRO
IT IS AN OFFENCE TO TO LEAVE LITTER

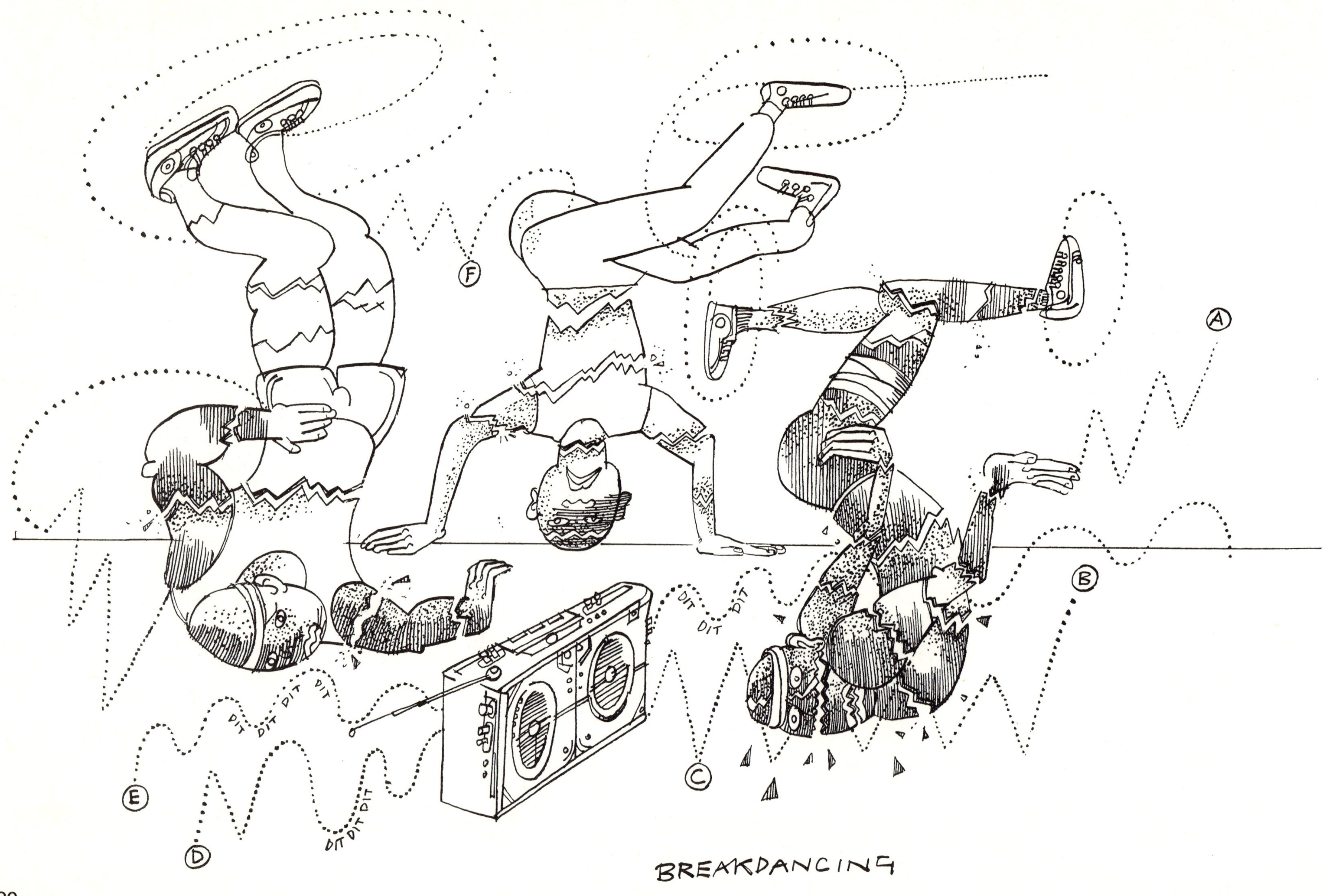
F
A
B
DIT
DIT
DIT
C
E
DIT DIT DIT DIT
D
DIT DIT DIT
BREAKDANCING

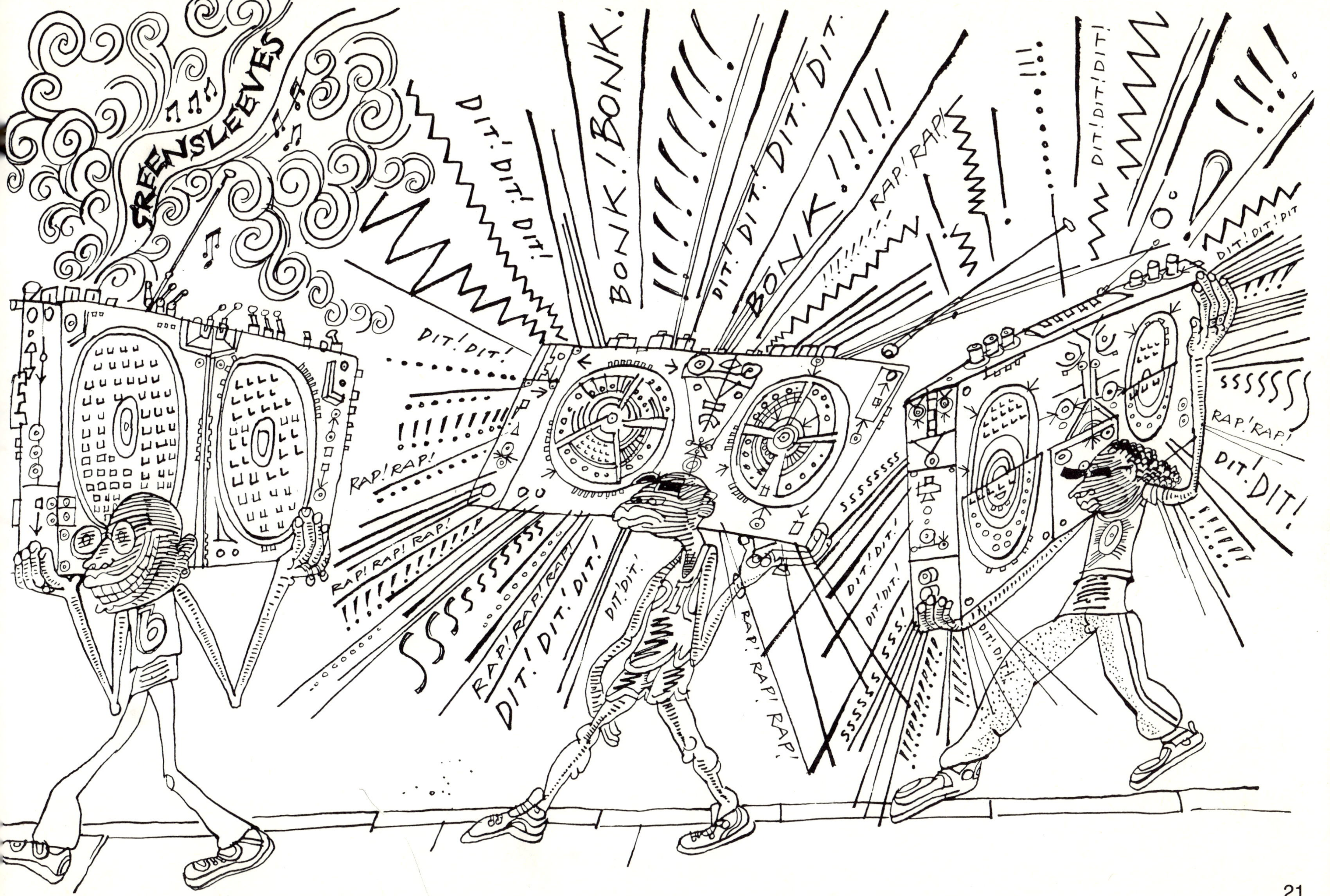
GREENSLEEVES
DIT! DIT! DIT! DIT!
BONK! BONK!
DIT! DIT! DIT! DIT!
BONK!!!!!
RAP! RAP! RAP!
DIT! DIT! DIT!
DIT! DIT!
RAP! RAP!
SSSSSS
RAP! RAP!
DIT! DIT!
RAP! RAP! RAP!
RAP! RAP! RAP!
DIT! DIT! DIT!
DIT! DIT!
RAP! RAP! RAP!
DIT! DIT!
DIT! DIT!

THE
DE LOREAN
TAPES

VOGUE

DIET
GASP!
GASP!
NIKE
NIKE

KEEPING FIT
CENTRAL PARK

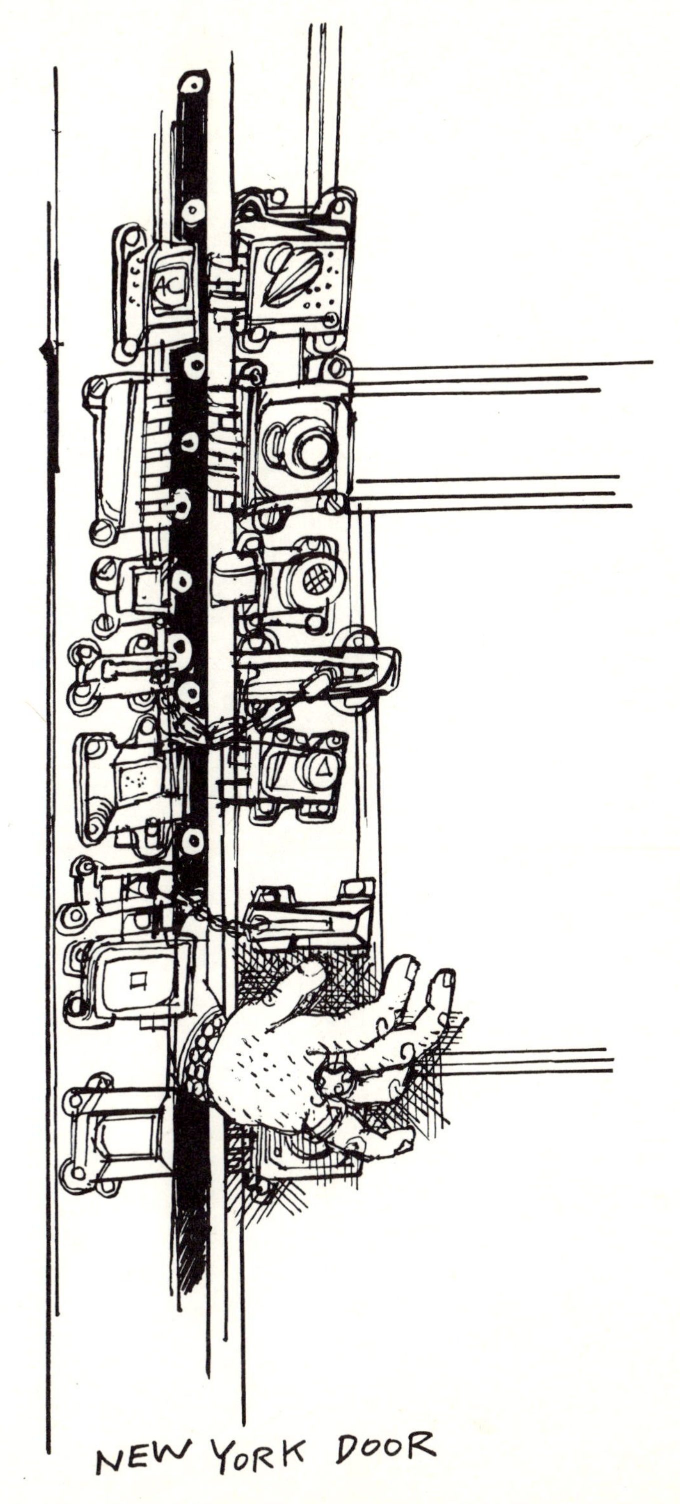

NEW YORK DOOR

GOING FOR IT!

YOU'VE GOT TO BE A SUCCESS!!
I'M NOT A SUCCESS
YES, YOU ARE, YOU'RE A SUCCESSFUL BUM
I'M A SUCCESS—I'M A RAT
I ALSO KEEP MYSELF UP TO THE LINE
I JOG EVERY DAY
BOY AM I FIT!
THIS GUY'S A SUCCESS! AND VERY VERY RICH!
HE'S GOT MORE MONEY THAN YOU HAVE—
LET'S GIVE HIM A BIG HAND
WOW!
EEEOWW!!
EEEEE OWOW
WOWWEE
ISN'T HE GREAT!
WHAT'S HE A SUCCESS AT?
IT DOESN'T MATTER! HE'S RICH!!

GOT ANY SMALL CHANGE?
GOT ANY SMALL CHANGE?
SMALL CHANGE!
GOT ANY CHANGE?
GOT..... ANY..... SMALL..... CHANGE.....
FREE ENTERPRISE

MAKING IT AVE
GO FOR IT AVE
THE MAINCHANCE St
SUCCESS
PALOOKAVILLE
BORN AGAIN St
FAILURE
GOT ANY SMALL CHANGE?

AMERICA ON THE MAKE
(GO FOR IT!)

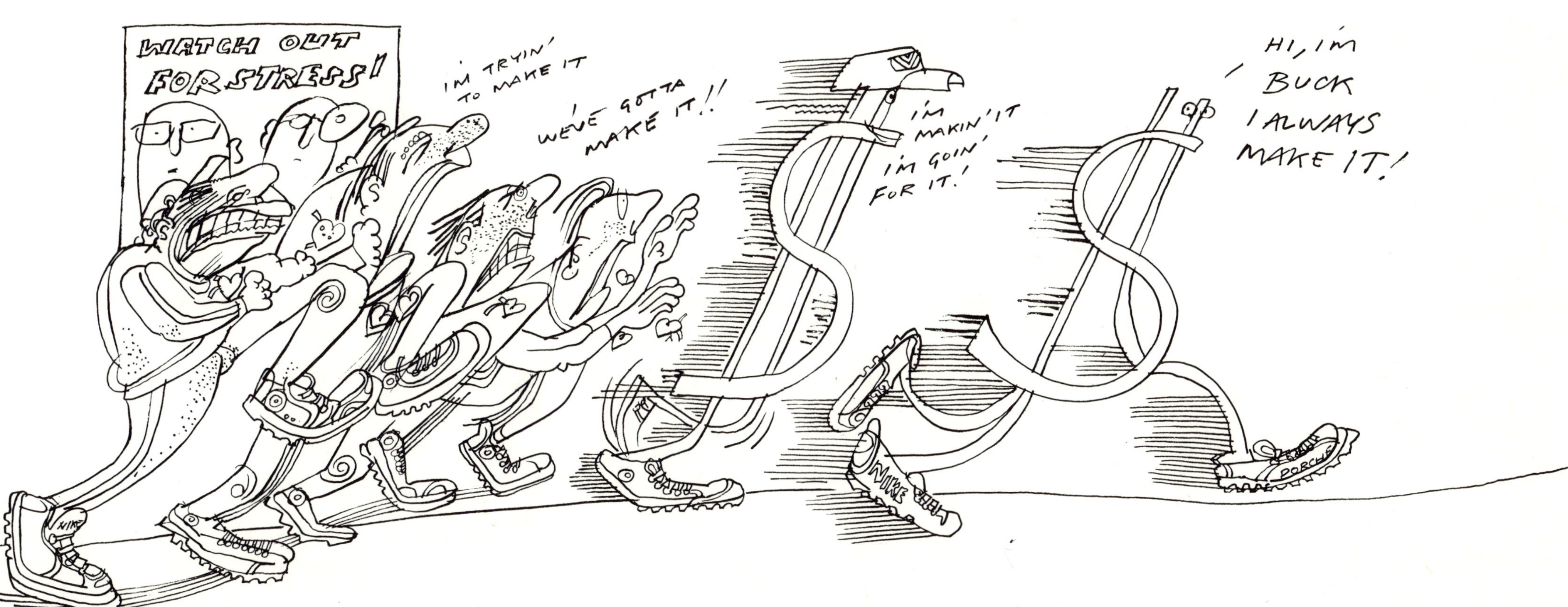
WATCH OUT FOR STRESS!
I'M TRYIN' TO MAKE IT
WE'VE GOTTA MAKE IT!!
I'M MAKIN' IT
I'M GOIN' FOR IT!
HI, I'M BUCK I ALWAYS MAKE IT!
NIKE
NIKE
PORCHE

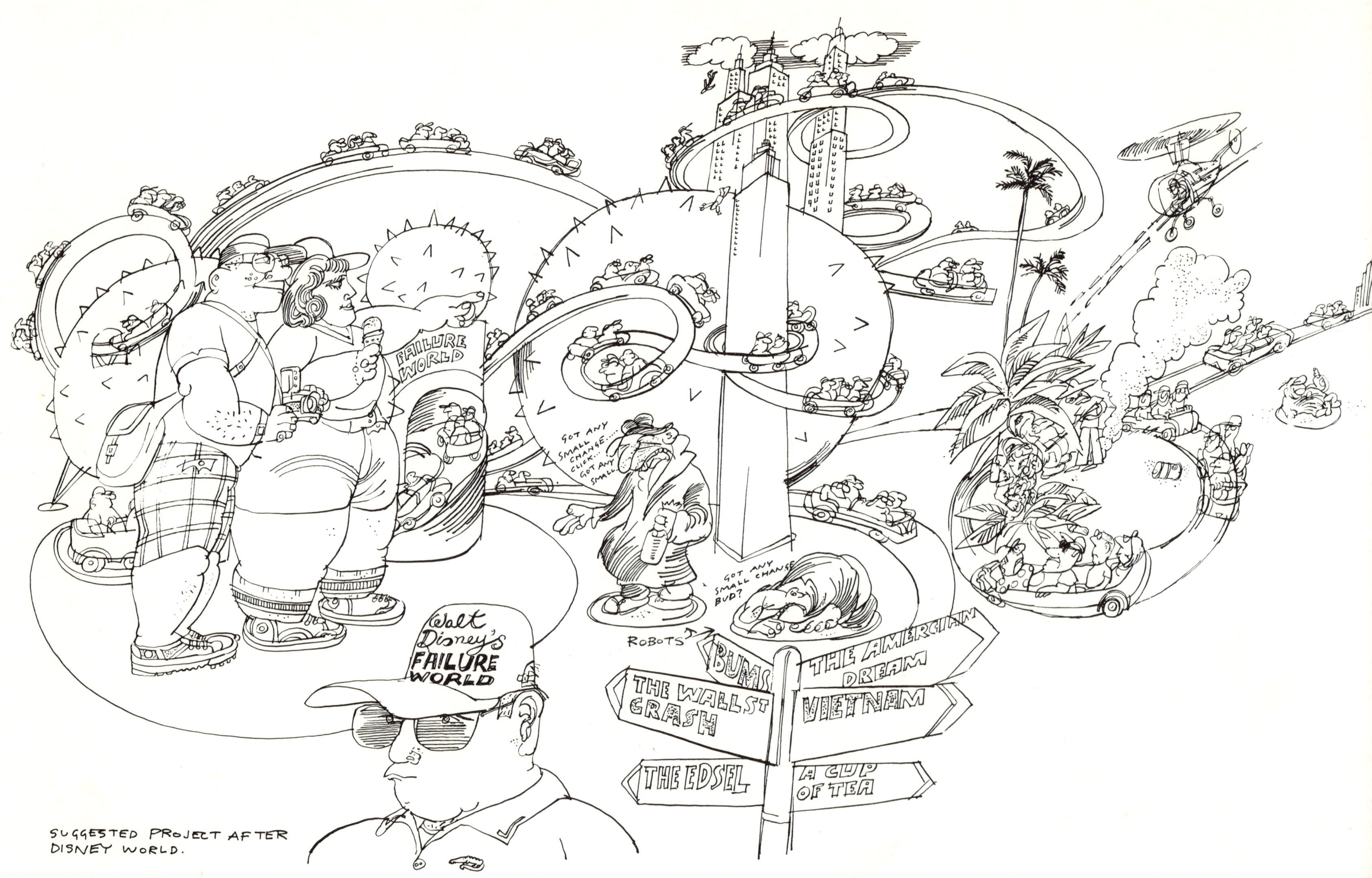

SUGGESTED PROJECT AFTER DISNEY WORLD.

YE OLDE BRITISH PUB
CLOSED
SALOON BAR
ENGLISH ALES
EPCOT CENTER
THEY SAY IT'S AUTHENTIC DOWN TO THE LAST DETAIL

GOIN' NOWHERE
REAL WORLD
THE RAT RACE
NOW SHOWING
DEATH OF A SALESMAN
BAR
BUMS OF THE PAST
GIVE US A BUCK ASSHOLE
CIVIL RIGHTS FUN WORLD
VIETNAM
PALOOKERVILLE
AIDS
WATER-GATE
THE AMERICAN DREAM
LOOK AWAY
LOST WEEKEND
NO CREDIT
UNSUCCESSFUL AMERICA
POLITICIANS ON THE TAKE (AND MAKE)
I CANT TREAT THE BUM- HE'S GOT NO MONEY
GOT ANY SMALL CHANGE
ROBOT

"HI! DAVE! WE WERE IN THE AREA, SO WE THOUGHT WE'D COME AND SEE HOW YOU WERE KEEPIN'"

HIGH-TECH AMERICA

SHOPPING MALL (DALLAS)

CHRISTINA'S WORLD
AFTER ANDREW WYETH

AMCO
AMCO
KICKING THE SHIT
OUT OF AMERICA
FOR A MORE
HORRIBLE TOMORROW
HAVE A NICE DAY!

REBUILDING
ATLANTIC
CITY

SPOT THE ENGLISHMAN
WHO THOUGHT HE COULD WALK

COMPUTER CONVENTION

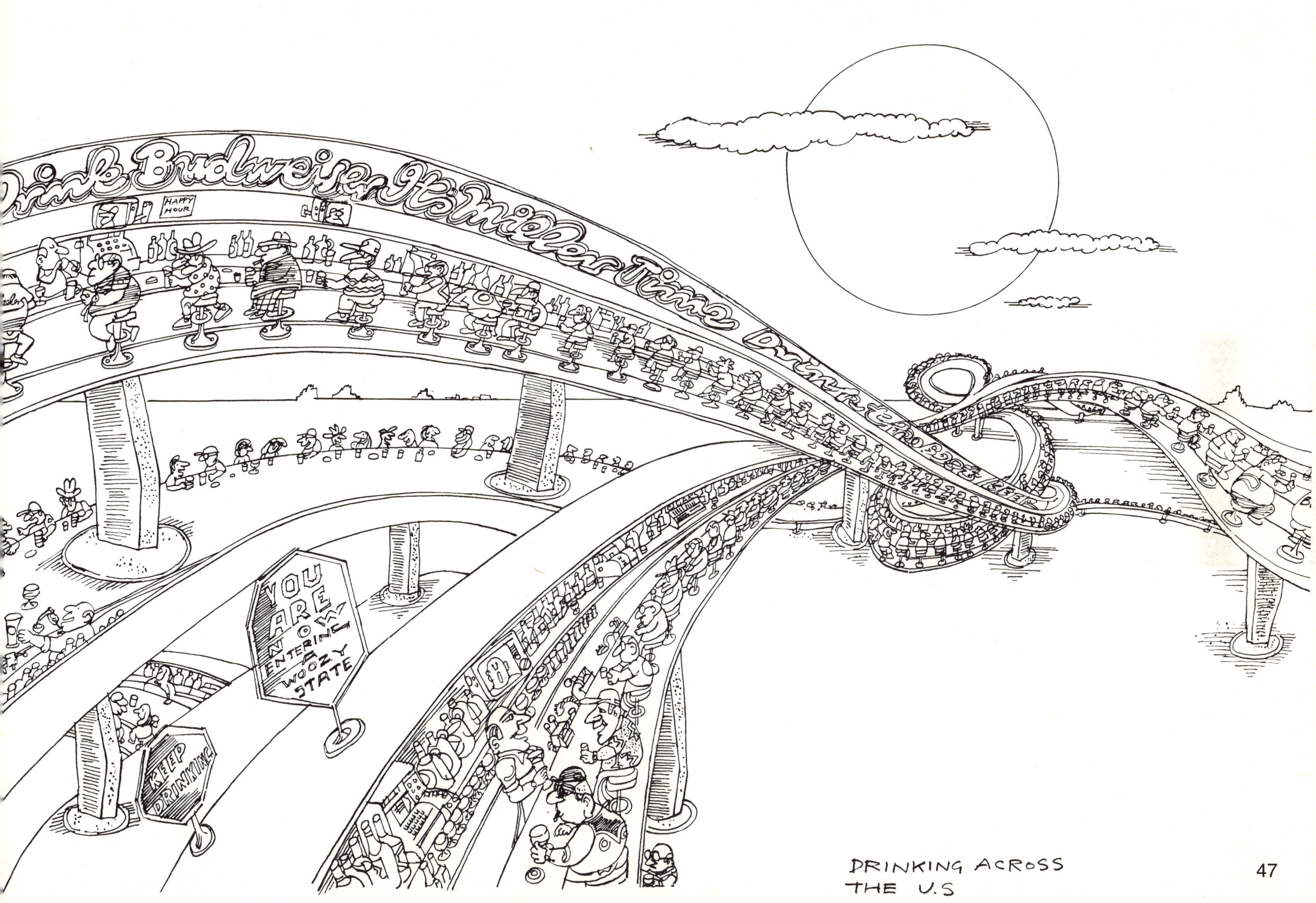

DRINKING ACROSS THE U.S

A QUIET SUMMER INDOORS
WITH ONLY THE AIR CONDITIONING
FOR COMPANY

IN BUILT AIR CONDITIONING WOULD
BE A GOOD IDEA

HITCHIN' A RIDE

DOWN SOUTH

BLUE GRASS
MOON PARTY

YOU KNOW WHAT IT'S LIKE
TO COME HOME TO AN EMPTY
COLD WATER APARTMENT TO
FIND THE ONE YOU LOVE
HAS GONE AN' LEFT
YOU ETC...ETC.....

A MAN'S BROKEN HEART
WILL NEVER MEND
IN THE EMPTY
ROOM OF MY
LOVE FOR YOU
ETC...ETC....

THE ENDLESS ROAD
IN MY HEART HAS
NO TURNING FROM
MY LOVE FOR
YOU

COUNTRY AN' WESTERN

Blue Grass
THIS NEXT SONG IS ABOUT A TRUCK DRIVIN' MAN. IT WILL SOUND JUST THE SAME AS ALL THE OTHER SONGS WE BEEN SINGING ALL EVENIN'
SO HERE WE GO FOR Y'ALL
FLASH
IN JAPAN WE ONLY HAVE YELLOW GRASS SINGERS
← JAPANESE FANS OF BLUE GRASS MUSIC

DOWN SOUTH

1899
TRADITIONAL $1
OTHER $2
THE SAINTS $5
Bourbon
BIENVILLE
GIRLS
Kate Sallers
GIFTS & CANDIES
NEW ORLEANS

AND AT THE END OF THE DAY THE SLAVES WOULD ALL SIT AROUND SINGING
COME ON
BABY BABY
RAP! RAP!
BABY
GET DOWN ON
BOOM!
BONK!
BABY
BABY
BABY
BOOM!
BOOM

SAVANNAH

FOOD

SELF MADE
AMERICANS

SLIMMING

DINER
I WAS WONDERING—
DO YOU DO A BOILED EGG?
I'LL HAVE BLUEBERRY
FLAPJACKS WITH
CHOCOLATE SAUCE
AN' MAPLE SYRUP
SUBSTITUTE AND
A SIDE ORDER OF
GRITS FOLLOWED
BY FOUR EGGS
OVER EASY WITH
HASH PLUS
GRITS WHEAT
AN' JELLY.......
SOURDOUGH.......
NO SALT!
BEE BEES
RESTAURANT
HAVE A NICE DAY
EGGS 'N' FLAPJACKS
EGGS 'N' BACON
EGGS 'N' EGGS
EGGS OVER EASY
EGGS AND MORE EGGS
SCRAMBLED EGGS
EGGS 'N' JELLY
HAM 'N' EGGS
HASH 'N' BROWNS
WITH EGGS

I'M STARVING!
EATS
HEATH NY

AMERICA IS VAST!

A BIGGER SPLASH PART ①

AN EVEN BIGGER
SPLASH PART ②

"NO ICE THANK YOU."

ENGLISHMAN IN BAR

SAY WHEN
Deli Deli
GD

REMEMBER FOLKS WITH THESE STRETCH NAPPY PANTS FOR ADULTS, YOU CAN EAT, WATCH TV, WITHOUT GOING TO THE BATHROOM!
IT'S TRUE FOLKS, I'VE BEEN HERE FOR THREE WEEKS
LITE

HAVE A NICE DAY
BOG MAC
FINGER
CHICK
GUM
POPCORN

LAS VEGAS

CIRCUS CIRCUS
HOTEL·CASINO
FREE CIRCUS ACTS
11 AM TO MIDNIGHT
ROOMS AVAILABLE
If not, we'll place you!
BREAKFAST BUFFET 45 ITEMS
BRUNCH BUFFET $2 45
LUNCH $2 50
RV PARK
FULL SERVICE
PIZZERIA
THE STEAKHOUSE
FAST FOODS
POKER
SLOTS-A-FUN
Riviere
SOLID GOLD
PROGRESSIVE
WINS WINSWINS
SLOTS SLOTS 'N' FUN
THE
WAGES of SIN
ARE
DEATH
HAVE A NICE DAY

PLAYTIME

RAIN COMES TO THE NEVADA DESERT (1)

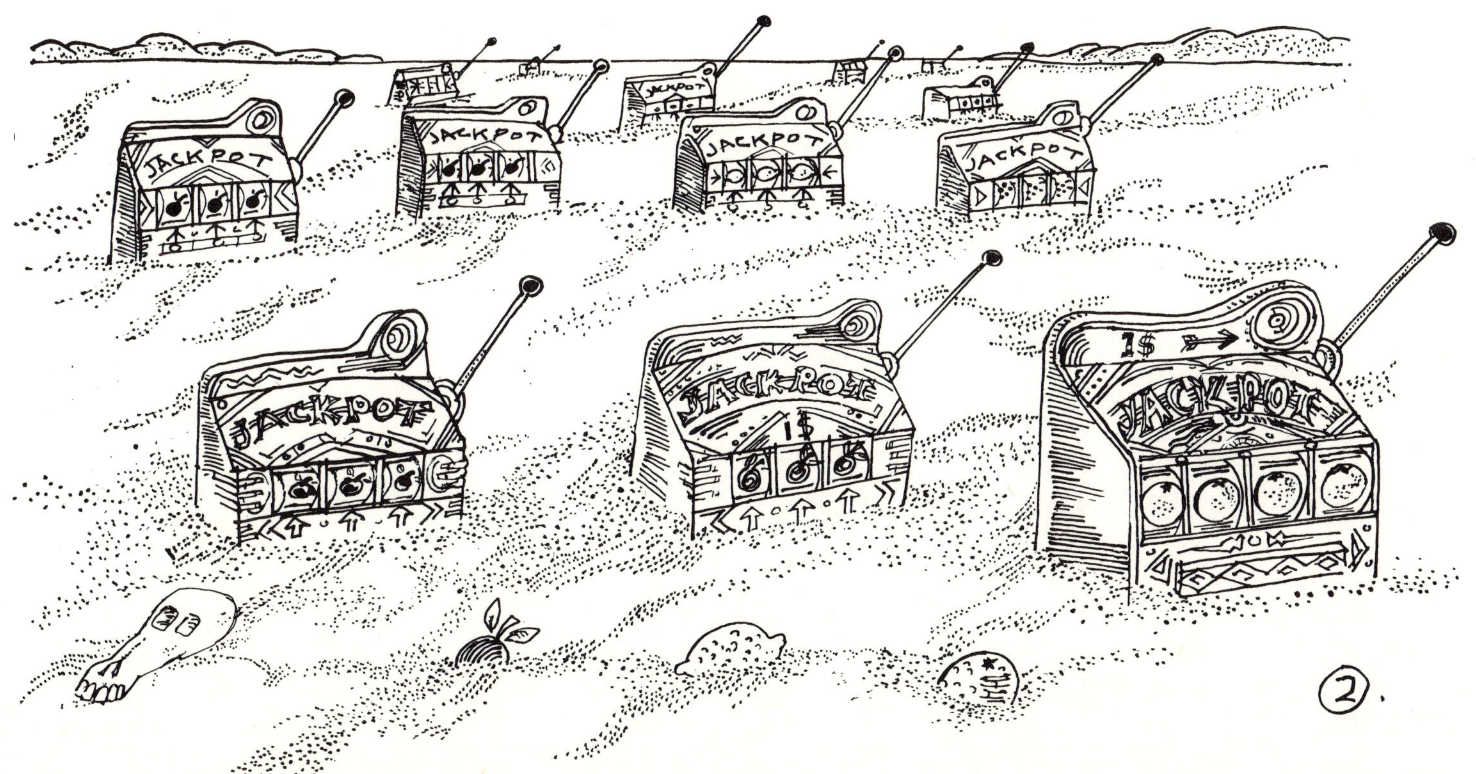
JACKPOT
JACKPOT
JACKPOT
JACKPOT
JACKPOT
JACKPOT
1$
1$
JACKPOT
②.

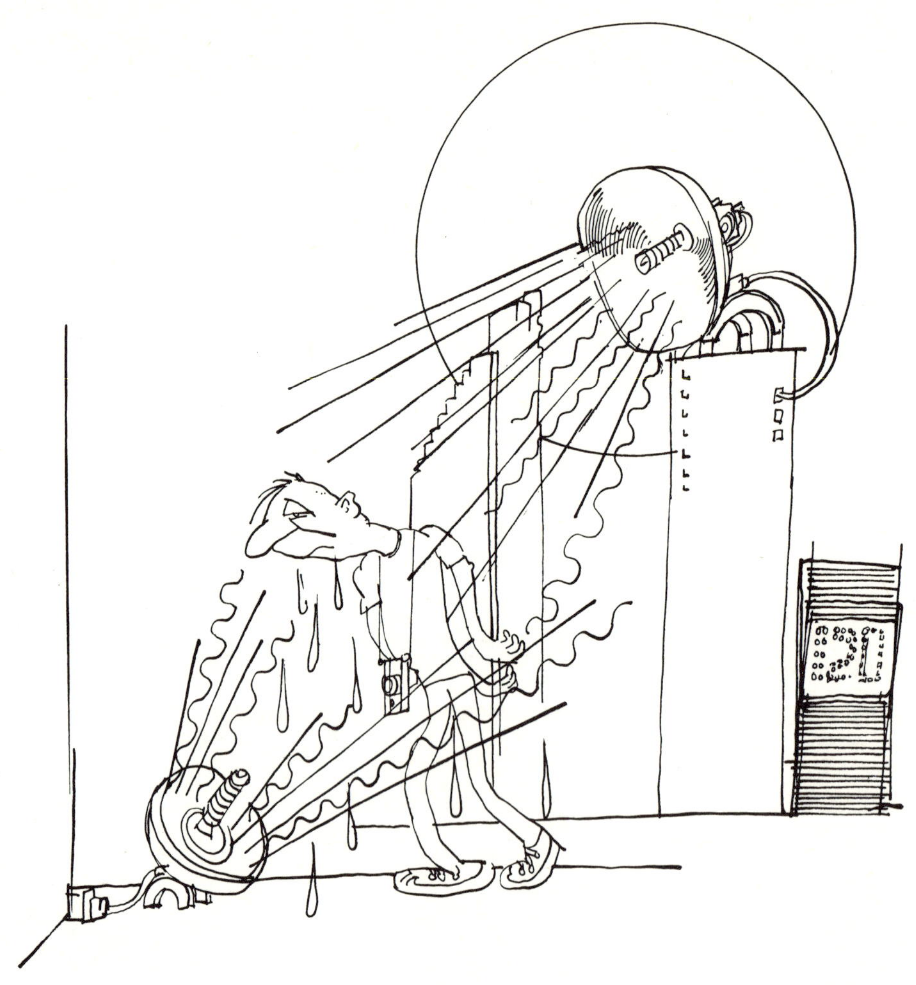

WELCOME TO VEGAS

CIRCUS CIRCUS HOTEL LAS VEGAS

SENSUOUS SOUNDS

intimate conversations
between consenting adults
"We live your fantasy"
Established 1974 24 Hours
Ask about *SENSUOUS STORIES*
(214) 69287467
or
(214) 369-88712

EDISON BELL RECEIVES THE FIRST DIRTY TELEPHONE CALL IN THE USA

EARLY SUNDAY MORNING 1985
AFTER EDWARD HOPPER

TYPICAL
DESERT
LANDSCAPE
NO WORDS COULD
DESCRIBE IT

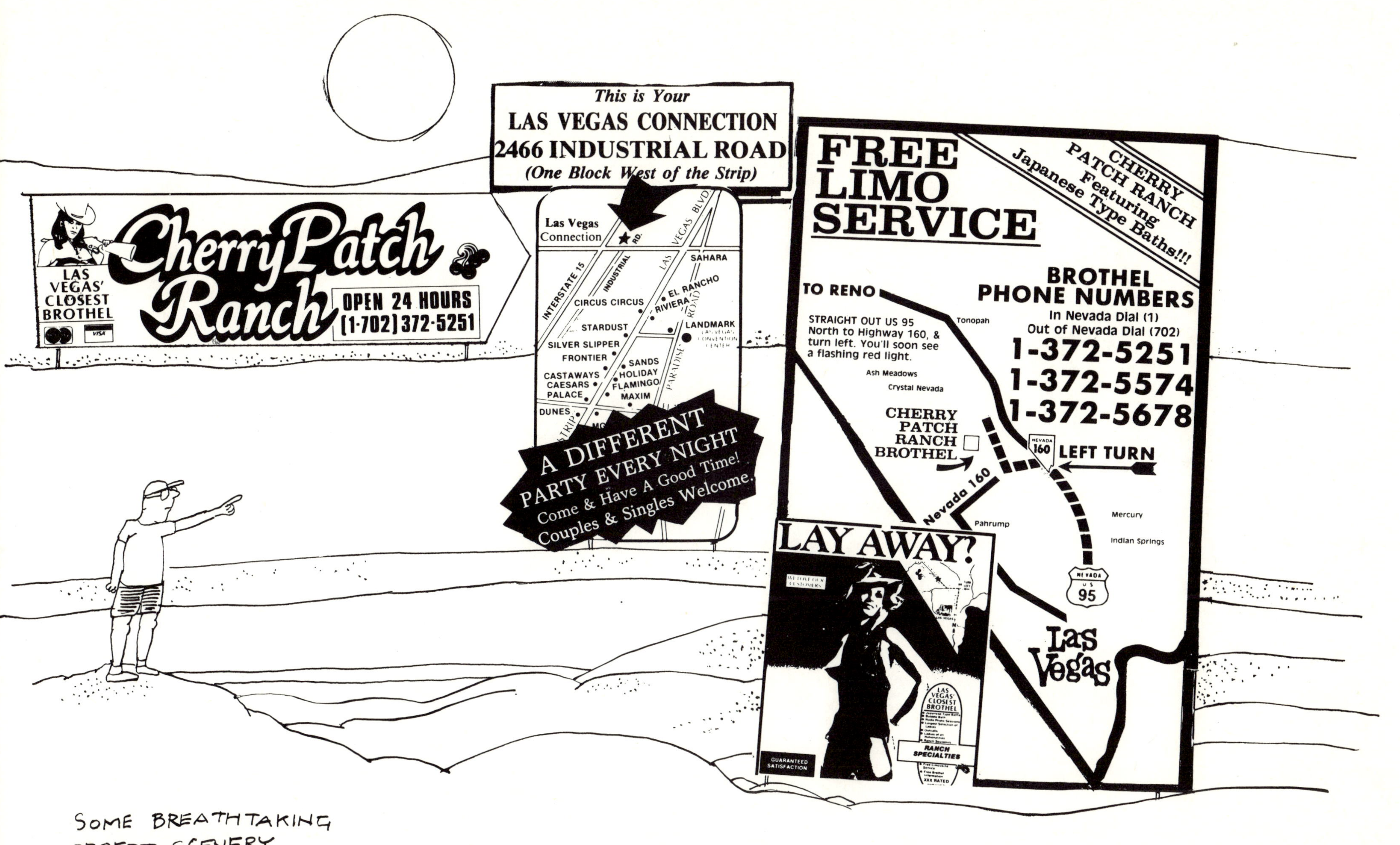

SOME BREATHTAKING DESERT SCENERY

A MORAL MAJORITY

SUNDAY MORNING

OF COURSE I BELIEVE THAT WHEN OUR LORD SAID THAT WE WOULD BE SAVED IF WE TURNED OUR HEARTS TO HIM ETC ETC..... MIND YOU WE ALL HAVE TO BEWARE OF COMMUNISTS WHO ARE TAKING OVER THE FREE WORLD...... IT WAS NICE MEETING WITH YOU SIR THIS IS MY WIFE MARY, WHOM I'M SURE WOULD ENJOY A MEETING WITH YOU..... MAY THE LORD BE WITH YOU......
MORMONS

A MAN BEING ANTI-AMERICAN

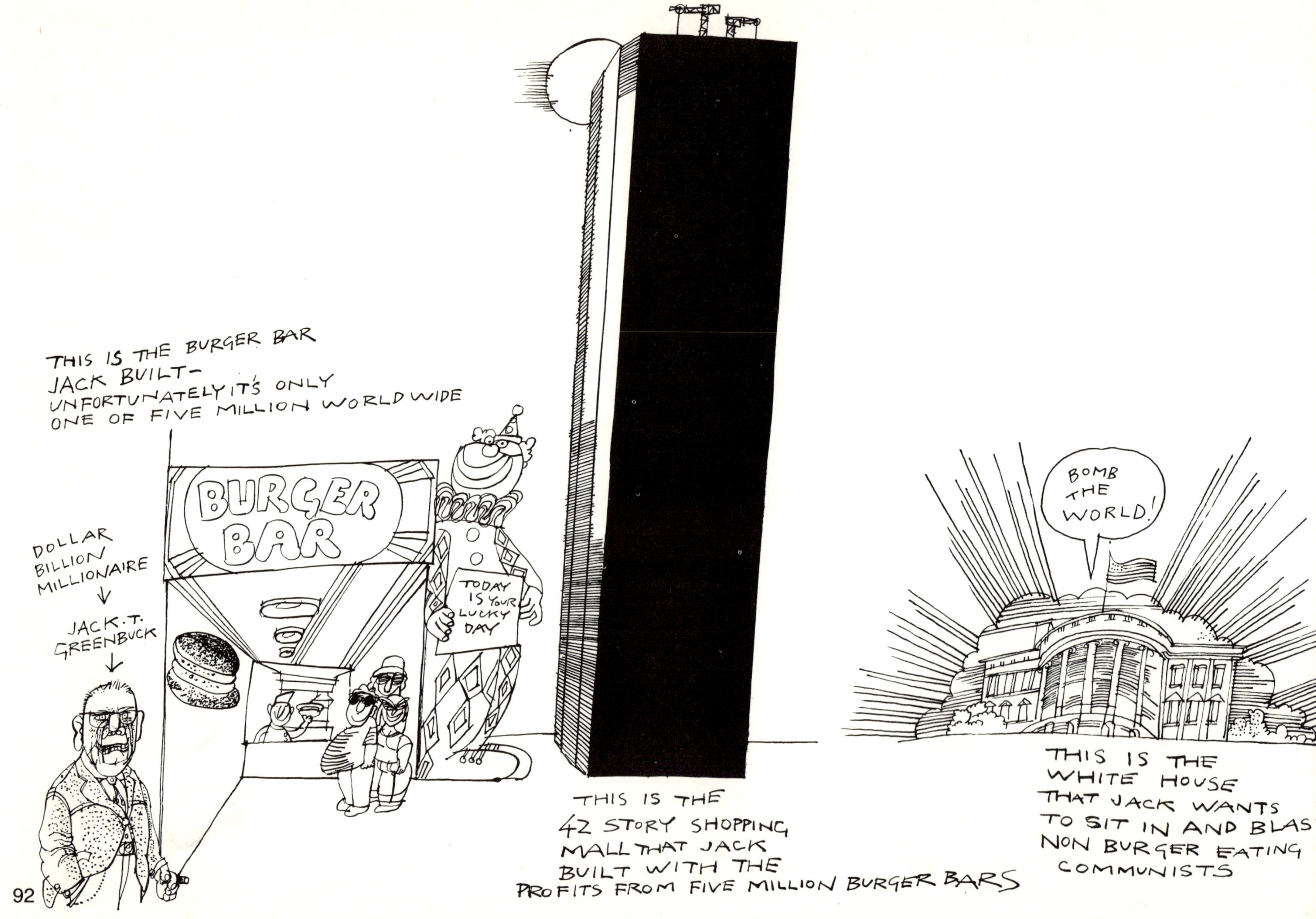
THIS IS THE BURGER BAR
JACK BUILT-
UNFORTUNATELY IT'S ONLY
ONE OF FIVE MILLION WORLDWIDE
BURGER BAR
TODAY IS YOUR LUCKY DAY
DOLLAR
BILLION
MILLIONAIRE
JACK. T. GREENBUCK
THIS IS THE
42 STORY SHOPPING
MALL THAT JACK
BUILT WITH THE
PROFITS FROM FIVE MILLION BURGER BARS
BOMB THE WORLD!
THIS IS THE
WHITE HOUSE
THAT JACK WANTS
TO SIT IN AND BLAS
NON BURGER EATING
COMMUNISTS

DRIVE IN
AN DI : E
COTE d'AZUR
LOOSE
4 HUNDRED
POUNDS
SAME DAY
MONEY BACK GUARANTEE
STEINBERG 65
STEINBERG 65
BURGER KING
PIX
TRAVEL
NO TRIPS
TO MOSCOW
ARRANGED
WELCOME
LOAN
SHOE
FIX
N

DECENT FOLK

3rd WORLD WAR
BOOM

HOLLYWOOD

HOLLYWOOD
EATS
GAS

MAPS
TO
STARS
HOMES
HOLLYWOOD

ISN'T THAT DAVE DIME THE MAN THAT PLAYS THE FRIEND OF THE BELL HOP IN THE T.V. SERIES 'TRASH'?
FANTASY TOURS HOLLYWOOD
FANTASY TOURS HOLLYWOOD
HOLLYWOOD HOMES
FANTASY

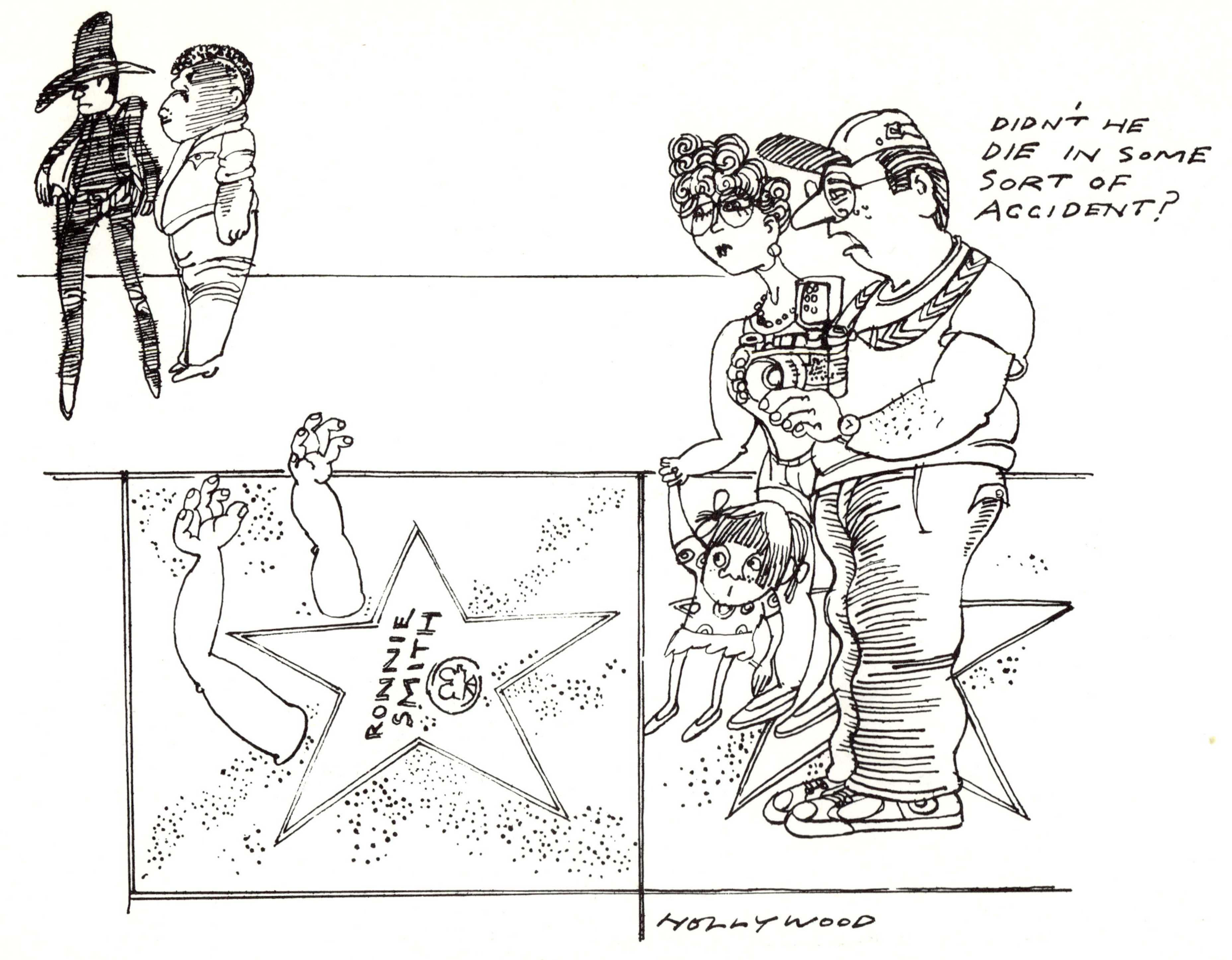
DIDN'T HE
DIE IN SOME
SORT OF
ACCIDENT?
RONNIE
SMITH
HOLLYWOOD

THEY SAY
IF YOU PUT AN
ASHTRAY TO YOUR
EAR YOU CAN
HEAR LOS ANGELES
SKATE BIKE

SAN FRANCISCO

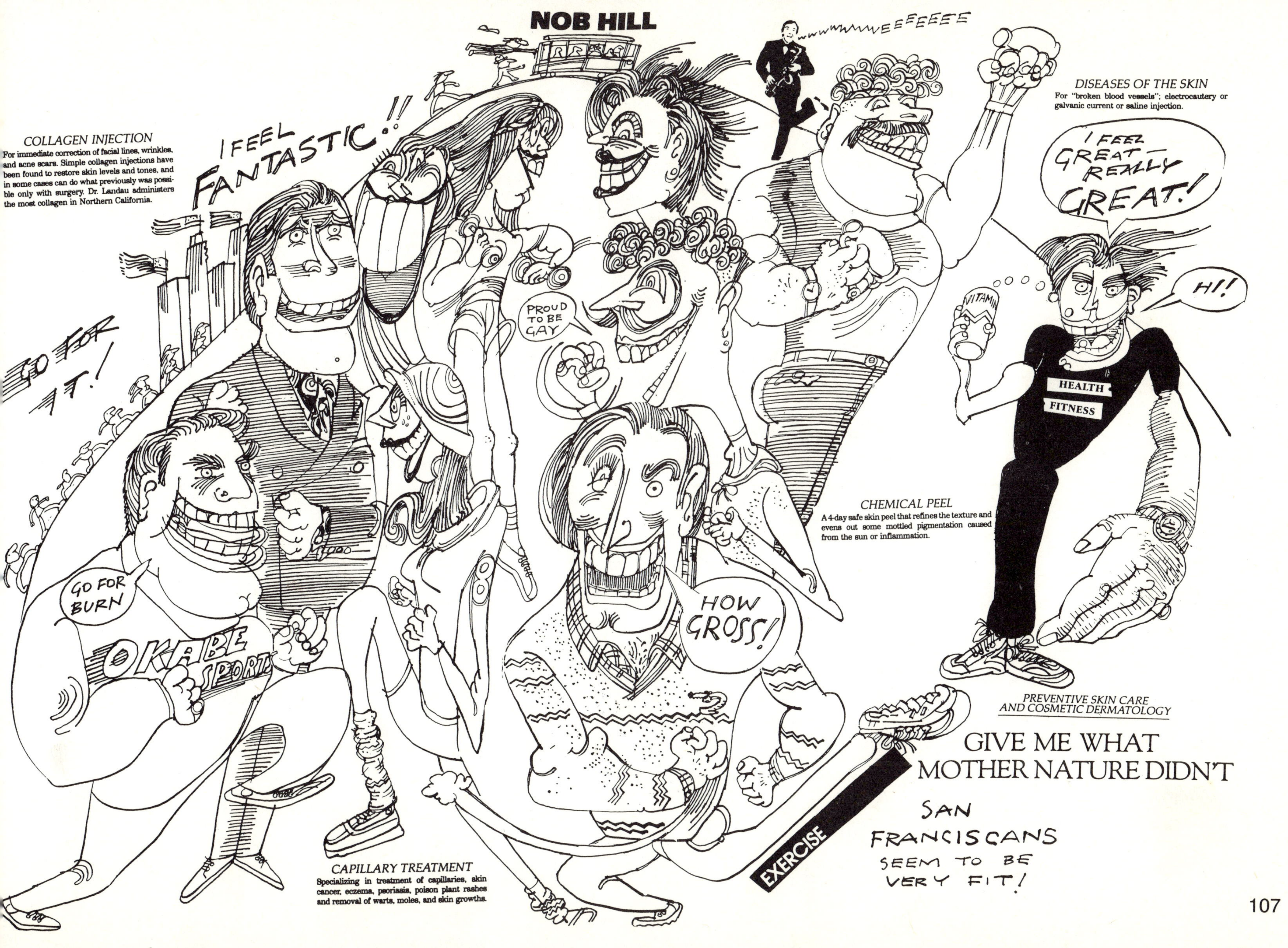
NOB HILL
WWWWWWWVEEEEEEE
COLLAGEN INJECTION
For immediate correction of facial lines, wrinkles, and acne scars. Simple collagen injections have been found to restore skin levels and tones, and in some cases can do what previously was possible only with surgery. Dr. Landau administers the most collagen in Northern California.
I FEEL FANTASTIC!!
DISEASES OF THE SKIN
For "broken blood vessels"; electrocautery or galvanic current or saline injection.
I FEEL GREAT— REALLY GREAT!
HI!
PROUD TO BE GAY
HEALTH
FITNESS
GO FOR IT!
GO FOR BURN
OKABE SPORT
HOW GROSS!
CHEMICAL PEEL
A 4-day safe skin peel that refines the texture and evens out some mottled pigmentation caused from the sun or inflammation.
PREVENTIVE SKIN CARE AND COSMETIC DERMATOLOGY
GIVE ME WHAT MOTHER NATURE DIDN'T
EXERCISE
SAN FRANCISCANS SEEM TO BE VERY FIT!
CAPILLARY TREATMENT
Specializing in treatment of capillaries, skin cancer, eczema, psoriasis, poison plant rashes and removal of warts, moles, and skin growths.

POWELL AND MARKET
FISHERMANS WHARF
3 BLOCKS
BAY AND TAYLOR

DING! DING!
506
POWELL
SAN FRANCISCO MAKES YOU FEEL SPECIAL

FOR RENT
PETE'S
CHINESE
LAUNDRY
DRY AND CLEEN
OPEN

I MEAN I SAID ARE WE INTO A RELATIONSHIP OR NOT? I HAVE THIS GREAT RELATIONSHIP WITH THIS GUY—I MEAN WHAT ARE WE TALKING ABOUT? I MEAN IT'S A ONE TO ONE RELATIONSHIP THERE'S NO CO-PILOT
I MEAN WHAT D'YER TALK ABOUT I MEAN WE TALKED ABOUT SEX HIS LIBIDO ITS CRAZY— RELATIONSHIPS ARE SO IMPORTANT— I MEAN EVERYONE SHOULD HAVE TO DO TESTS— YOU HAVE TO SEARCH— TALK TO EACH OTHER EVERY DAY ONE TO ONE
EXCHANGE BAR SPECIAL
IMPERIAL CALVERT
$1.20

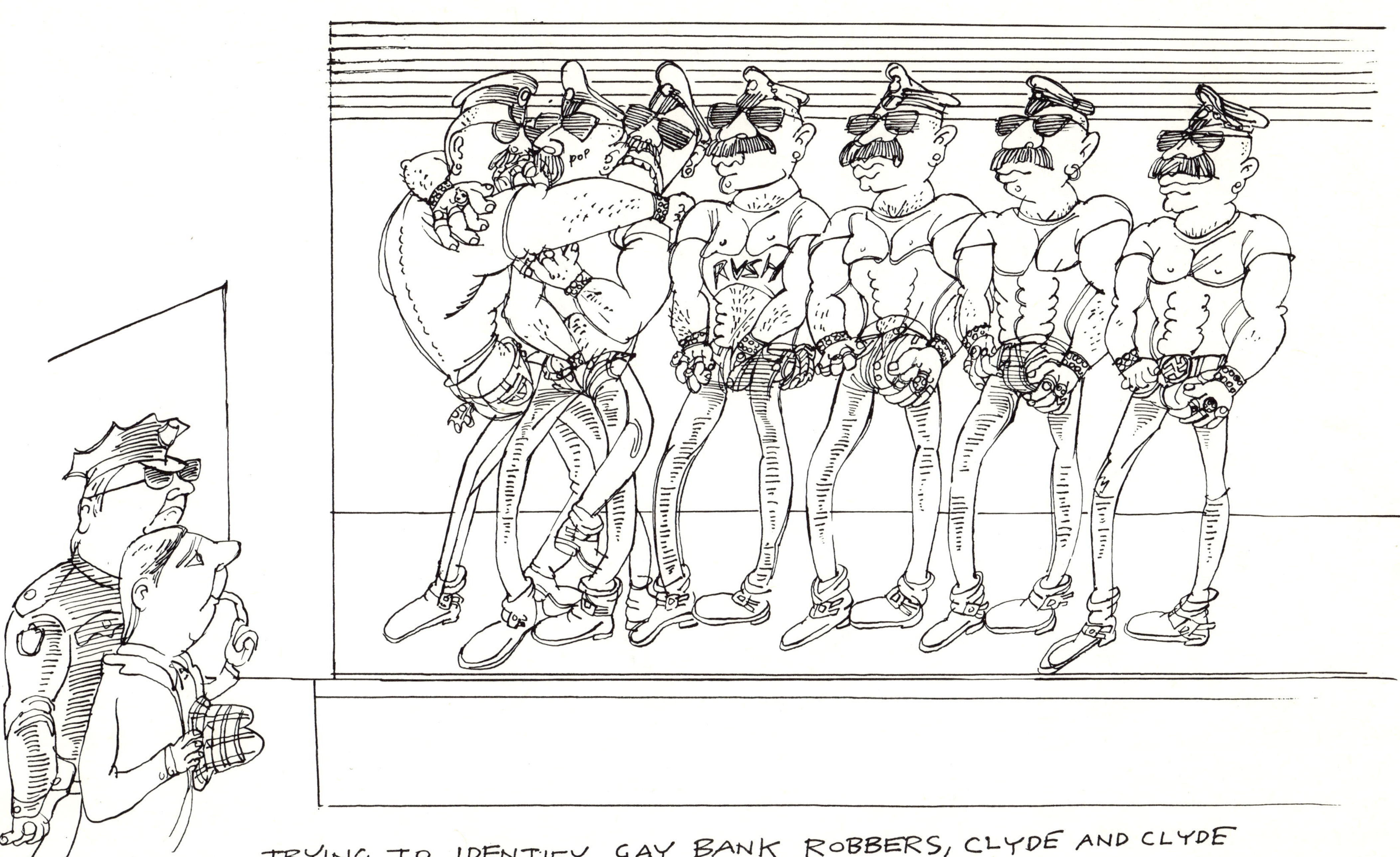

TRYING TO IDENTIFY GAY BANK ROBBERS, CLYDE AND CLYDE

I'M LOOKING FOR A FRIEND – HE'S WEARING DARK GLASSES A TEE SHIRT AND HAS GOT A MOUSTACHE

LAW AND ORDER

HAVE YOU
GOT THE
TIME
PLEASE?

I THINK WE'RE BEING HELD UP BY SOME CRAZED KID!

HEY HONKY!
LEAVE HIM ALONE SIR-PLEASE!
JOE DOAKS
NOW LISTEN SIR, THIS IS A DECENT LAW ABIDING CITIZEN!
COMMON OUT PUNK!
LET ME AT HIM, I WANNA MUG HIM! I'LL KILL HIM!
GUARDIAN ANGELS

GANG ROAST POODLE
LOOSE 400lbs OVER NIGHT
NIGHTMARE KILLS TEEN
NEWS
TEEN DELIVERS BIGFOOT BABY
HOUSEWIFE COMMITS SUICIDE IN HER DISHWASHER
CRIPPLE'S AN EVIL GENIUS
QUADRIPLEGIC IS ACCUSED OF MURDER
HED RATHER STEAL A NICKEL THAN EARN A DIME
BILL
OUR SON WAS REBORN AS DOG SAY GRIEVING PARENTS
BURIED WOMAN WAKES IN COFFIN

SIGNING OFF

iv United States
UNITED STATES
freeway
BRITISH COLUMBIA
ALBERTA
SASKATCHEWAN
ONTARIO
QUEBEC
NORTH DAKOTA
NEVADA
UTAH
NEW MEXICO
LOUISIANA
NEW YORK
NOVA SCOTIA
VANCOUVER
SAN FRANCISCO
SAN JOSE
SAN DIEGO
DENVER
MONTREAL
PORTLAND
BOSTON
NORFOLK
ATLANTA
JACKSONVILLE
NEW ORLEANS
MIAMI
ST PETERSBURG
CIUDAD JUAREZ
MONTERREY
NATIONAL MONUMENTS

Michael Heath was born in 1935 in London. One of Britain's most popular and accomplished cartoonists, he is a regular contributor to the *Sunday Times*, the *Standard* and the *Guardian*, and for many years his cartoons have been the mainstay of *Punch* and *Private Eye*. Always the first to recognize a new trend, a new style or the joke in a seemingly serious event, Michael Heath is a unique chronicler of his times. He is married and has two children.